DEMYSTIFYING YOUR SPIRITUALITY

SOME SIMPLE WAYS TO GROW HEALTHY BODY, MIND AND SOUL

BOSCO EKKA

Contents

Contents

Preface

Slowly, over time, you become more spiritual. If you get hurt or have an out-of-body experience, this process can be sped up. As a group, we have felt like we were separated from God or source, and we have looked for God outside of ourselves. By going inside, that inner voice is strengthened and has more of an impact on our lives. There is no such thing as good or bad; only experience and lessons are real things that happen. We all have intuition, but we can choose whether or not to listen to it or not.

The more we work on that connection, the stronger it will be. This will help us connect more with our spirit and higher self. Some people use meditation, which helps them connect with and get help from the universe on a regular basis. If we do something, we will get back what we put out. This is called the law of cause and effect. What we think of as luck is often the result of something you did that made you feel good and paid off. As long as we have a good life, we could become aloof or lazy.

Spirit may help move you out of harm's way if it isn't your time to leave this world. We are here to help our souls grow and change. Our job is to learn how to quiet our egos and balance them with the nudges of the spirit. Materialism may be a big problem for spiritual growth. I've come to understand that the goal of life is to grow spiritually through the teachings we choose on a soul level before we were born.

We might be able to learn more about our soul's nature if we know more about our past lives. In some ways, channelling has the power to fill in the gaps in parts of our society that we are still not aware of or haven't found yet.

We live in a world that has many different realities and viewpoints, but most people don't live in a world that has a lot of different dimensions. It is best to keep only what you like or agree with and get rid of the rest. There are astral entities who enjoy lying about being this or that ascended master when they are not.

The best way to learn is to learn how to get information from your higher self or I AM presence. I hope that some of this information about channelling and discernment will help you as you move forward on your spiritual path. A good way to start is by contacting or going to a Spiritualist church in your area, or by taking development classes at a well-known school or institution. I began to think about freedom and what it was like to be free. I think it's important to look at your life and think about what it will take to be free and happy.

Some things in life can't be changed, but our perspective can always be changed. Developing discernment is an important part of rising through the ranks. They are often souls who have risen before on other worlds or at other times on Earth and are now here to show humanity how to do the same. They want to show people how to do the same. You can see a lot of signs of ascension. Some of them are very mild, and others are very bad. One of the most obvious signs is that you become more sensitive and psychic.

If you are empathic, it may be hard to spend a lot of time with certain people or groups of people. Spend more time outside, swim, and bathe in water to clean your body and aura. The myth that as one rises, one doesn't die, and thus becomes body immortal. This is a common misconception about ascension. There's a better chance that you'll live longer if you go up in vibration more.

As you rise, you can get into the storehouse or akash of your higher self and other lives. In general, the more one rises, the more active and efficient one's body and DNA become. To stop taking medicine without talking to your doctor could be dangerous. This is even more true if you have an illness that needs it. One of the benefits of ascending is that you become more aware of how your mind, body, and spirit all work together. You also have a better sense of what you need to do to rebalance.

Many people spend a lot of time thinking about themselves and their close relationships. They value relationships that will make them happy and money, as well as things, experiences, and sensory pleasures. People and goods don't make you happy or peaceful when you have them. The human race has done a lot of bad things in the past, and the current pain in the world is a result. How many people spend even a small amount of their time expressing gratitude and love for our beautiful planet?

Earth and her natural spirits are loved by many people. People love them because they work so hard to give us everything we need. Many people in the world only think about themselves and their own selfish wants and goals. They are cut off from their heart and probably don't want to be there. Giving love to the earth seems like a bad idea. They don't even think about it.

The fifth element is called Akasha, which is also called The Spirit, God, Emptiness, The Divine, The Source, The Infinite Light, The Great Mother, and the Force. It is also called the fifth element. : This spirit has no self, no time or space, no attachment, no ego, no desire, and no negativity: infinite joy and unfathomable love and kindness are all it has to offer us. You don't have to be there; you just have to be aware of everything. This love changes us into who we are. Give this love to everyone because this chalice shows that the source of love is always flowing out to everyone and everything.

Always, you know that the Universe's infinite creative force is coursing through every cell of your body, giving life to your whole body. All the time! OF YOUR LONG-TERM! Everything moves into, through, and as it. You live your life the way you think, feel, and believe.

What you think about yourself is how your life will turn out. If you want to change the direction of your life, start by changing how you speak to yourself. Each person has the right to get everything that life has to offer. Until each one of us has it! In whatever way one thinks is best for oneself!

Start with yourself. This means that you are in charge of everything that happens in your life and that you are in charge of your reality. As you know, the world is not out there. It is a picture of something inside that is happening outside. And it all starts with you.

Unless you start to think and feel in a different way more often, nothing will change. The more you think the same way, the faster your reality will change for you. Define and get clear on what you want to achieve, no matter what it is. Keep your focus on the desired outcome like a laser beam. Keep your attention. It will happen.

You are making whatever you believe, no matter how big or small it is! You can learn about anything you want. In our world, there is no way around that. Bring your ideas to a logical end. Are you going to let those scary ideas make you crazy?

There is no point in being a kook, so come to your senses. Kali Yuga: This is what Eastern esotericists call this era, and it's when things get dark the darkest. The Aquarian age is coming and things are going to get bright again. Great laws of rebirth, Karma, and the development of individuals and countries will come to be known and accepted in the coming years. People now believe that the inner essence of man, the existence of the soul, and psychic abilities in all of their many forms are scientific facts. There are more and more people who don't like traditional religion.

In this time, we can choose to align ourselves with the good and pure, the Aquarian violet fire energies. This is the time when we can choose to align ourselves with these forces. I saw in my vision that one day, humans will be able to learn everything they need to know on their own, and it will come from inside, like a living library. In time, people who were on the spiritual path would move in a different direction. There will be a shift in the way people think and feel as their consciousness and vibration rise. People will want to help, teach, and inspire instead of just trying to stay alive. Humanity would set up new privacy agreements between relationships so that no one could find out about the thoughts and feelings of intimate partners.

Some parents even downplayed the importance of our wants in their thoughts to make them feel better about not being able to make more money. Our basic desires and emotions may have been thought to be bad as we grew up in a lot of different ways, though. As adults, we become dissatisfied because we don't understand why we have so much trouble making love and making money. The best way to meet more of our current needs is to appreciate them rather than hate them or downplay their significance. This way, we can meet more of our needs. When we look inside at our inner self-image, we think about the things we've learned and done in the past.

The world is full of love, and if we just let it, it can come out at any time. It will be easier for you to get what you want if you can love all of your wants and see yourself as deserving of having them met. Things about us no longer bother us as much when we look inside ourselves, and we don't care as much about how we look as we did before. Let's look inside ourselves, see how beautiful we are, and find everything we've been looking for but haven't found. Our awareness allows us to find the best parts of ourselves, our inner power, and our ability to change for the better.

Let's change our inner image in a way that makes us feel better on the inside and gives us the strength to resist temptations that weaken our confidence every day. Let us be open to the love we have inside us and not smother it, but instead embrace it as a positive force that clears away old debris that has hid our centre from us. Our core is an important part of life because it unlocks our God-given inner abilities, which allow us to embrace ourselves. Philosophically, it's a question of whether or not to be who we are. But it's also a symbol of self-love, which lets us become who we truly are and decide that we don't want to return. Keep from looking back.

Old things make us want to go down old roads, but inner love lets us find out what we want in our hearts. Be open to new experiences and challenges that will help us find inner peace and let go of the past. Striking a good balance between spirituality and pleasure. Because I think that life should be fun, I let myself have a lot of fun things. As someone who has had this happen to them, I know that when I give myself these things and feel good about them, I don't feel the need to overindulge.

There are times when this kind of meditation can be useful, though. For example, when you have a real addiction to something, something you can't stop yourself from having a lot of. In this case, if your favourite thing is chocolate, you'll eat yourself to death. It didn't seem right to me. I decided to stop taking part in this meditation. Some people think that if you don't do things that you enjoy, you become more spiritual.

Trying to be more or less spiritual doesn't make you more or less spiritual in my opinion. I think that we should enjoy our lives, not lessen them because of our spiritual journey. This is very important to understand, because if you think that all pleasures are bad for your health, you have a very skewed view of spirituality.

We don't usually plan out the most epic trips in advance. They tend to come together over a few months or years or even decades. What would it be like to have complete confidence in ourselves, our environment, and our place in the world and in what we do? There is no sense of self-consciousness or feeling like an outsider, because there is no one to look up to. How would that look? I don't know what you mean, but I think it would be like serenity; personal peace.

As a child, I think we're all beautiful. But as we get older, we get worn down and lose sight of our own unique strength. When I've been an adult, I've forgotten about my own strength. A big part of our job in this life is to protect our inner light and keep that inner flame from dying out completely. The world needs both my light and yours. When I hit rock bottom, there was no mask I could wear, no denial, and no way to hide the truth.

For the first time in my life, I realised that I didn't have the strength to fight. Accepting any help or comfort that was given to me made me wonder if I had been feeling love up until this point. Everything changed after months of going through all of this. People should remember that not all awakenings are peaceful. When compassion is present, blame starts to fade away.

Without guilt, there is no need for forgiveness. I wish I could remember when I first felt love on my trip. I knew within a day or two that it had happened because I felt lightheaded, euphoric, calm, and something I can only describe as my chest expanding. Even though I was shocked, I did not think it was a big deal. The answer is love.

I'm sure of this, too. Your "inner voice," which has a lot of knowledge, and "the mean little voice," which doesn't have a lot of knowledge, both have a lot of other parts. By acknowledging their existence, acknowledging their intelligence, and acknowledging that they are there for your protection, love and care as well as your growth, you can start to accept and love them right away. Self-acceptance is the process of seeing and accepting who you are, even if you don't think you're good or bad. It's also the process of not judging your own self. How does it work? When someone is who they are, you become more patient and kind to him or her.

Silence helps us see our lives and hearts as they are. It is in this state of profound stillness that one learns to control his or her own life and destiny over time. The best way to avoid making mistakes that could kill you is to use your gift of inspiration in a smart way. People have life and intelligence because of the "Mind and Consciousness of God," which is what gives them these things. Slowly, over time, you become more spiritual. If you get hurt or have an out-of-body experience, this process can be sped up.

As a group, we have felt like we were separated from God or source, and we have looked for God outside of ourselves. By going inside, that inner voice is strengthened and has more of an impact on our lives. Each of us has the power to make good changes in our lives. Through our ideas, words, and actions, the universe responds to us in a way that we can see and feel in the world. During hard times, it is normal to question God or your religion. It is very natural to do so. This is how people are.

In other words, if you can look at the situation objectively, you will get more clarity and insight into the situation Change your reality from one of victimhood to one of power. If we do something, we will get back what we put out. This is called the law of cause and effect. What we think of as luck is often the result of something you did that made you feel good and paid off. Because we are powerful, it is better to focus on the good things in our lives rather than on what is wrong or missing.

There are some who think that the things we call "errors" are actually instructions or efforts to save someone's life. I don't think there are any mistakes in life. I think that no matter what we do, we always learn something from it. What does this mean? If it isn't your time to leave this world, spirits can help by making things like traffic jams to move you out of the way.

1

The Surrendering Art

Concentrating on oneself is a deeply entrenched concept in our environment. The whole capitalist system is predicated on individuals adopting a self-centred perspective on life. Even new age spiritual beliefs emphasize themes such as discovering oneself, who one is, and divine sovereignty.

Many who consider donating do so only in the human race—contributing to society and assisting other humans. Alternatively, we may go so far as to help other creatures if we have compassion for them. It is all excellent. It's great to shift our attention away from ourselves and onto others.

Many individuals, on the other hand, are preoccupied with themselves and their intimate connections. They prioritize the relationships that will bring them happiness and money, material things, experiences, and sensory pleasures.

The issue with this self-centred attitude is that when things go wrong, as they always do due to excessive self-focus, we may feel extreme stress, fear, anxiety, worry, despair, and a variety of other emotional issues.

There is nothing wrong with wanting happiness and desiring harmony, which is precisely what pleasure is: the harmonious functioning of the human being's mind, body, and soul. Yet, our approach to happiness, whether via relationships, money, or other external factors, is destined to fail. Accumulating goods and people do not produce pleasure or peace.

Many individuals are fearful and anxious about themselves and their futures. It is not uncommon for people to be stressed out about money and financial circumstances. Dealing with work and relationship issues may be very challenging. Not to mention sickness, disease, and psychological difficulties. And these are those that are lucky. At the very least, they are not hungry or subjected to slavery or war, as many others are.

All of these dangerous circumstances and issues arise as a consequence of human beings‘ previous deeds. The human species has committed many atrocities throughout history, and the present suffering in the world is a consequence, apart from the many atrocities committed by people against one another, animals, and the environment. We continue to deplete our magnificent planet's resources without providing anything in return.

It is a narcissistic exaggeration of our species' selfishness, which depletes the planet's body and mind without providing anything in return. We think that this world is ours, oblivious to the fact that we are all beneficiaries. Everything we have, including our belongings and beings, is a gift from the planet's awareness.

And how can we repay her? How many individuals devote even a tiny portion of their time to expressing appreciation and love for our beautiful planet? Who loves Mother Earth and her natural spirits, who work tirelessly to provide us with everything we have? The magnificent energies that surround us on our planet are one-of-a-kind and wondrous in the universe. These convey their affection for the divine creatures who govern our world, the elementals of the sea, sky, and soil. That honours the planet's beauty and the love that pervades everything. What do we do with the creatures that emit this love incessantly?

No, many members of the human race only see themselves, their selfish wants and goals. Giving affection to the earth seems irrational. Indeed, it is not even a thought that occurs to them. What we can grab and take. How much money am I proficient in earning? How am I to "survive"? Who is going to adore me? How am I to be content? How much profit am I capable of making? How can I progress my standard of living? How am I made up to care for my family? How do I find a partner?

The greatest strength a human being has is their capacity for love. Giving this love is the purpose and manifestation of existence on our planet. Gaia does not need your money, and all of your things already belong to her; they will be returned to her when the human species is reduced to the dust of an old memory. Gaia yearns for the human race's love, compassion, and innocence.

To radiate love from the heart and aura to all creatures on this planet. There is nothing to fear, and there is no need to "attempt" to survive. When your thoughts, feelings, and emissions radiate love to all of mother earth's manifestations. Our language of love, of communing with and connecting with nature via attachment, is what this civilization's human people need. As a consequence, they are shut off from the heart and likely dread it.

Our planet and all other planets and galaxies in this universe were formed out of nothingness to commemorate love. It is the magnificence of harmony. You reach this state of peace via the heart and mind's outpouring of love. This way, you become a part of the global celebration of love.

The world's suffering is a result of previous bad karma. Compassion and love generate enormous quantities of good karma in the present and future. There is no better technique to build your meritocracy than this (that is, the actual treasure that continues not only for this lifetime but for future generations).

The fifth element is Akasha. Others refer to it as The Spirit, God, Emptiness, The Divine, The Source, The Infinite Light, The Great Mother, and The Force. It is the endless emptiness that gave birth to all of existence. This spirit is void; it has no self, no time or space, no attachment, no ego, no desire, and negativity: infinite joy and unfathomable love and compassion.

Spend time meditating to let go of attachments, anxieties, desires, appetites, tensions, fears, and self-obsessions. Allow ourselves to let go of the things that constitute our identity and disintegrate our ego into limitless nothingness. There is no such thing as a self there; just pure awareness exists. We enter Akasha and transform into a chalice filled with love. Our identity is transformed into this love. Give this love to everyone since this chalice represents the perpetual outpouring of the source of love to all beings and things.

There is nothing to fear or worry yourself about. All of our requirements are fulfilled. Whatever difficulties we face, wisdom, understanding, and solutions emerge from the boundless depths of love and the great spirit. When we are consumed with ego and anxiety, our fear obstructs the flow of energy through us. Allow yourself to be free of stress and uncertainty. This frequency is synonymous with complete confidence and faith. Allow the almighty source's infinite knowledge to flow through you.

We shall all perish one day. At some point, the human species will vanish from this world. And not long after that, the planet will pass. All of our fears and anxieties will be in vain. All that remains are our expressions of appreciation and love for one another, the earth, and the almighty. It will continue in perpetuity. As a result, forgive and forget all those who have mistreated you.

To live a beautiful and harmonious existence and to enter the holy place of eternal peace and pleasure. Allow love to fill the heart, mind, and soul.

2

Each item is a Single Item

Bear in mind that these are individuals. Everything is a solitary entity. And everything comes from one thing. Furthermore, there is ONLY ONE Thing.

We can walk around in circles for the rest of our lives, bumping into things and shouting no to something, all the while pretending that we "have no clue what's going on out there?" While the bulk of our attention is focused on our fears and anxieties about ourselves and our surroundings, We may continue playing the ignorant game while pacifying our dissatisfaction with another movie, some more food, another cigarette, another bowl, or another drink.

While we are aware that it is a fabrication, We are all aware that there is much more to life than feeding our cravings and keeping the economy afloat. And this bizarre corporate machine about which none of us is concerned. We've continued to do so because everyone else has. And everyone who has come before us has always done so, and we have all just agreed that "this is just what you do!" What else could you possibly do?

There is always the knowledge that the Universe's Infinite Creative Force is coursing through every cell of your body, animating your whole existence! At all times! Of your PERMANENT! Experiential learning. You are breathing life into your physical body and animating every element of it. Everything is flowing into, through, and as it.

There is always the reality that your body is pumping a vibratory signal across the Universe at this moment, and at all times, that is the culmination of all you think, feel, and believe about your environment. Additionally, since this signal is a vibration, it is magnetic and attracts additional vibrational passwords in tune with it. As a result, YOU become the PRIMARY Influencer of what occurs in your life.

You are the engine that propels your life forward. Not your work, the economy, your degree, family, government, or anything else. Your ideas, feelings, and beliefs shape your signal, which in turn shapes your life. Your life unfolds following the thoughts, emotions, and opinions you have. Whatever self-talk you're having in your mind, that is how your life will develop. If you want to alter the course of your life, begin by changing the way you speak to yourself. You are the chauffeur.

It may be difficult. It's unquestionably more convenient to continue bouncing around, wondering why things are occurring and when they're going to change. It's far more convenient to get up each day and do the same thing we did yesterday while wondering where all the change has gone. Every day, we reaffirm our lunacy. Repetition of the same actions with the expectation of a different result is acceptable. What more could we possibly do? We had no idea of any better. That is how my mother did it, and that is how the instructor and preacher did it. That is the method they taught me. And everyone on television is doing it! What more could I possibly do? That is acceptable. It takes a great deal of courage to switch off the world and live your new truth. You can, however.

Indeed, it is most likely why you came here. To LIVE your new truth and serve as an example to others. That is, the world needs our intervention! If we are to succeed! At any point in life. Naturally, we do! We all want to live rich lives, and I'm sure we all wish that everyone else does as well. Each human being is entitled to everything that life has to give. And we can have it all! We will all have it one by one until each one of us has it! In whatever manner one considers appropriate for oneself! And it all begins with the singularity. It all starts with YOU. "

You are the source of everything that occurs in your experience, and you are capable of creating wonderful, pleasant, happy, and uplifting events to happen in your life. And you deserve to have wonderful, content, and uplifting events occur in your life. You are deserving of the best life has to offer. Additionally, you can build one for yourself because YOU are the creator of your reality and the author of your experience! The world does not exist "out there," as you are well aware. It is a reflection of an internal activity that is occurring "out there." And it begins with you. Your world starts on the inside!

You are accountable for using your constant ideas and emotions to direct and form your world. Nothing will change unless you begin to think and feel differently more often. The objective is to be present at all times. The more constant your thinking pattern is, the more quickly your reality will alter for you. You must be consistent and concise. Wishful thinking results in a wishful experience.

The more concentrated and constant your thoughts are, the more quickly your reality will change.

Define and get clear on what you are attempting to achieve (regardless of it) and maintain a laser-like concentration on the desired result. Allow nothing to distract you from your concentrated purpose. Every day from now on, be laser-focused and crystal clear on your objectives. or motives, or anything. Allow nothing except encouragement and confirmation to speak to you even if the process takes a year. Nobody ever fails at anything; they give up. Maintain your concentration! It WILL occur! " I assure you. I've seen it work far too many times to have any remaining reservations. And I've discovered that the distinguishing element is the ability to maintain the vision through time. It would be best if you kept your eye regardless of what occurs or how much time passes. Maintain your concentration. It WILL occur! "

It may take some time. It may need some practice. And you have access to every tool necessary to get started. ATTACHED Your mind is one of the most powerful powers in all of existence. I think that is not hyperbole. When the concentrated reason is constantly at work, miracles are frequent. Additionally, this gadget is always working for you!

It rambles on all day, every day, on various topics that may or may not have anything to do with what is occurring! And the majority of the time, it's about nothing that's happening. All of this is speculative, based on hypothetical situations that you would almost certainly avoid if given the option. Whichever way you look at it, your creative energy is at work. What are you currently creating? Throughout the day. Every single day. Your ideas are resonating across the Universe, contributing to the whole of All-That-Is.

Particularly in one's own life.

Additionally, collectively. Not to mention the fact that the very ideas resonate throughout your body, affecting the activity and reproduction of your cells. (it is a separate article).

You have the option of underestimating the power of your ideas if you so choose. You may continue telling yourself that "it's too difficult" or that "you're incapable of doing it." You "previously attempted that, and it failed." Inform yourself about anything you want. You are the creator. There is no getting around that in our world. You are creating whatever you believe, whether it is limited or limitless! Acknowledge this. Recognize this? WHATEVER YOU THINK Whatever you feel, whatever you believe, You are the creator.

You have it! Make a statement! It is your choice; do what you want. And if you want anything else, go ahead and get it! Approach it even if it is just a passing notion because your thinking acts as the spark. And you are aware that this is true! It is time to begin living as if it were true. Bring your ideas to a logical conclusion—rope in your rambling thoughts. Are you going to allow those fear-filled ideas to drive you insane and into poverty? Come on, you kook, come to your senses!

YOUR MIND IS THE ONE WHO DIRECTS YOUR LIFE. Put it to use.

We must attempt. We don't want to continue receiving what we have been receiving, do we? It is past time for us to move on. The old thing is tedious, and it's not making us any happier. It is past time for us to start thinking and feeling our way toward a new world. A world in which we have all realized our mind's vast, limitless capabilities. In such a world, everyone understands the power of their thoughts, and we are all focused on getting the best possible result for ourselves and everyone else in our world. And with a thought, we have altered the course of history.

PEACE, LOVE, AND ACCEPTANCE ARE THE KEYWORDS.

3

The Inner Reality

For endless centuries, despite the numerous attempts of negative forces and powers to extinguish its light, the truth of man's inner, spiritual essence has persisted. Through ages and epochs of absolute darkness, despair, and devastation, the flame has been maintained by people with the ability to see beyond the thick curtain of the physical, material world.

In the enormous cycle of man's development, epochs of darkness and devastation are followed by generations of light and advancement, with the cosmic pendulum and cosmic law determining seasons and periods.

Mankind has passed the point of deepest darkness in this era, which the Eastern esotericists refer to as Kali Yuga, and is rising once more with the arrival of the Aquarian age.

The bloodshed and devastation, the conflicts and economic turmoil that have engulfed the world are just the last stages of the Pisces era's demise. However, as with all things that expire, there is a tenacious clinging to the old and outworn, to outdated, crystallized ideas and attitudes, and this is true of man's nature as a spiritual/material being as well.

Orthodox, secular religion continues to have a tremendous grip on men's and women's views worldwide. Those who are willing to explore with an open mind remain a minority. However, chinks and holes are beginning to emerge more often in the thick veil of the secular world, allowing the light of the one truth to shine through, and this will continue to increase as mankind progresses further into this Aquarian era. The realities of the great laws of rebirth, Karma, and the cycles of development of individuals and countries will come to be recognized and acknowledged, and mankind will finally come of age and join into the conscious brotherhood of the universe, of man's oneness with all that is, with this global reawakening. However, one must be practical and recognize that this state of relative perfection still lies far in the future. When we consider the ongoing wars, increasing violence, oppression, dire poverty and hunger, and economic chaos, it is not difficult to see how far ahead this wonderful spiritual time still lies.

Nonetheless, the process has started. It began with the twentieth century, which brought a large number of great souls into incarnation whose spiritual/material/technical labour on various levels aided in raising mankind and setting it on the path to real-life spiritual liberation.

This state is now emerging in organizations formed in reaction to the Aquarian influence to study and explore the esoteric, meditate and pray, and discover their pathways of contribution to their brothers. A paradigm shift in awareness has been used to describe this worldwide movement or swing away from the established, the conventional. The inner essence of man, the existence of the soul, and psychic abilities in their many manifestations are now widely accepted as scientific facts.

Self-actualization and self-realization are concepts that refer to actual states or circumstances of being. An increasing number of souls are unhappy and disappointed with traditional religion, with blind faith, dogma, separatism, and tyranny. Without a doubt, a massive movement toward unification is underway throughout the world, a recognition that people everywhere are the same, with the same hopes, desires, and yearnings for freedom, and that the only hope for this tiny world is global peace, goodwill, and resource sharing, and that above all, we are one humanity.

This globalization of mankind is unprecedented in human history; in fact, our globe is often referred to as a "global village." We are truly living in THE CHANGE OF CHANGE, a time when we can consciously align with the energies and forces of the good and pure, the Aquarian violet fire energies. The moment has come for mankind to advance towards a genuinely beautiful and noble future.

4

Living Libraries-Humanity's Future

I got a glimpse of humanity's likely future and the direction we are collectively headed the other night, shortly before falling asleep. This vision came to me as a download of knowledge, which I then translated into words. The next section delves into my imagination and the download I got.

At the moment, humanity heavily depends on external knowledge, whether it is contacting a doctor for health advice, doing Internet searches, or visiting a local library or bookstore. There is an abundance of information available for you to seek out and investigate. I was shown in my vision that mankind would ultimately internalize the knowledge they need, and it would come from inside, basically transforming into a living library. Humans would be able to obtain knowledge from the inside rather than from the outside. This may manifest as instantaneous knowledge, the ability to access the akashic records or the ability to channel information from one's higher self and guides.

While some individuals currently possess this capacity, the primary distinction I heard was that someday, everyone would be able to do so. Along with the ability to obtain any knowledge desired, people would develop an increasing capacity for telepathy. You would be able to deduce not just what someone is thinking but also how they feel. As a result, the spoken phrase will progressively lose significance. Humanity would establish new privacy agreements between partnerships to ensure that no one probes the thoughts and emotions. This would create a unique and more personal connection between lovers, family, and friends in more intimate interactions.

According to my understanding, people on the spiritual path would make a gradual shift. Depending on the individual's consciousness and spiritual talents, there will be different degrees of telepathy and channeling. As humanity's consciousness and vibration increase, there will be a shift away from the virtual drive to survive and toward the desire to heal, educate, and inspire. People will increasingly pursue their interests and abandon professions and relationships that no longer offer them pleasure. These changes are already taking place for individuals on the spiritual path and are paving the way for others trailing behind.

It's going to be an amazing trip, but not without its own set of unique obstacles. I was given a general timeframe for this, but it is also contingent on humanity's collective readiness for these changes. For some, these changes are already underway; for others, they may take many years. What is clear is that, contrary to appearances, mankind and the planet Earth are developing and changing from the inside. I'll conclude with this proverb, which I believe sums up this essay perfectly: "if you don't go inside, you go without."

5

Acceptance of Our Human Needs Without Condition

So many of us learned to ignore our fundamental human needs as children, believing we were helping others or avoiding emotions of shame, guilt, or humiliation. This started for some of us even before we could speak.

Our diaper required changing, and this was seen as repulsive. Our pleas for affection and attention were dismissed as a nuisance, and our nutritional requirements were seen as a burden. And how many of us suffered due to our family's predictions of poverty, as our demands were seen as a drain on the family's resources?

Some parents even downplayed our wants' significance in their thoughts to alleviate their guilt about their inability to materialize more money. There are many ways in which our fundamental desires and emotions may have been despised as we grew up, which was very demanding on our morale.

A kid can only take so much anger and poverty projection until the adult world's inequality becomes apparent. We begin to hate our own needs due to how they affect others and the projected reaction. Isn't it preferable to have no desires at all than to be despised?

Then, as adults, we become dissatisfied without understanding why we have such difficulty generating love and prosperity. We are so used to ignoring our desires for love and nurturing that we wonder why we don't attract what we want in life.

I had a stunning realization last month when I realized that the rejection experiences I had throughout my adolescent years were a direct reflection of how I had rejected humanity when I was eleven years old, resulting from an abusive affair with a teacher the subsequent emotional neglect.

At the time, this was the straw that broke the camel's back for me. I abandoned mankind and determined that I would have to fend for myself since I could not trust the adult world to support my life's mission. Some part of me rejected everyone, and that rejection returned in the form of the resonance I was carrying. I faced rejection at every turn, and it was only now that I understood the world was attempting to reveal who I was. It's incredible how that works!

As a result, much of the lack of abundant flow we feel reflects an element of our inner state of being, some of which dates back to infancy. We are drawn to the mirror image of our resonance. This is the law of nature.

Thus, the answer to meeting more of our current needs is to appreciate them rather than hate them or minimize their importance. It may have been easier in a certain context to minimize our wants or to reject them entirely, but this serves no one in the present.

People even attract abusive relationships in the modern-day due to these ingrained kinds of denial in which we believe we are undeserving of love. Occasionally, we need a reminder that we decided to embody anger and denial of our fundamental needs for love and nurturing until we see the strength of our agreement and begin affirming something else.

Begin now by developing a greater appreciation for your requirements. Love that you need and are deserving of. Recognize any underlying denial of your wishes. Recognize where you made yourself "less than" to avoid being abused by another's projections.

"I am deserving of love." "Like everyone else, my desire for love and nurturing makes me human." "I am as worthy as an innocent, newborn infant of being loved, hugged, and provided with all I need to flourish." "I am just as worthy as the rest of the world."

The more you can love all of your wants and view yourself as deserving of having them met, the faster new portals to love and abundance will open up inside you. Your body and mind were created to connect to the universe's love and quantity, and there are portals of receptivity inside you that may have been shut off in the past when your needs were not met.

Now you must accept responsibility for meeting those demands, and when you do it emotionally, you will attract a mirror image of your resonance. There is an endless supply of love ready to be released if we just let it.

"I am deserving of receiving." Be appreciative of your human needs. They are not a stumbling block. They are not an impediment. They are a component of your manifesting capacity, and you have come here to understand your full ability. You have come to undo the old humanity's programming and embody the radiant love of the new humanity until the benefits of honey and abundance that flow to you overflow into the lives of all those around you. Each of us is deserving of unconditional love. Abundance is a fundamental human right.

6

Image of one's Inside Self

When we look inside at our inner self-image, we reflect on our previous experiences and realizations. Realization liberates us from all of our prior beliefs and enables us to live a more fulfilling future.

When we open inside ourselves, into our inner being, our external appearance ceases to matter, and things about ourselves end to worry us as much as they did before. For instance, if we were previously dissatisfied with our looks, we now see that appearance is just a shell and that our inner worth makes us valuable. Let us look inside, realize our inner beauty, and discover all we've been searching for but haven't found. Our awareness enables us to uncover the highest aspects of ourselves, our inner power, and our capacity to change for the better in any area we want to improve. When we shut ourselves off and flee from difficulties, we go farther and further away from our core. Because assisting others in need provides us with tremendous inner strength and kindness. We should not coerce people into accepting our assistance since they will not be appreciative enough. We should strive to be nice even when everyone else is gone and believe in the self-realization that comes with silence and serenity.

When we look inside our inner being, we are approaching the moment of our truth that has been plaguing us for a long time but has been repressed on the inside and not expressed. Accepting oneself is very tough, yet it eliminates our arrogance and haughtiness when we do not embrace ourselves. Our inner image assists us in creating and fulfilling all of our dreams and expectations since when we look inside and discover inner power, things flow more easily. This is because we've drawn attention to our environment, which has unlocked all the previously blocked doors due to our self-consciousness. When we choose to achieve all of our desires, our inner strength, which is a component of our confidence, enables us to encounter individuals who may assist us in gaining new insights into ourselves and reestablishing internal equilibrium. When we reject our inner self-image and fail to acknowledge it as our essence and core, we deny our outward self-image.

Let us be at ease with our only body. Additionally, we should strive to keep our bodies functioning properly. Our inner power teaches us how to behave effectively in every circumstance. Our bodies communicate in a million ways what they are carrying, but we ignore these signals as long as we do not look inside. Our ideas and anxieties impose a weight on our bodies as well, if they do not originate in our heart, in the essence of our being. Our core changes daily if we are not on the correct road, one of inner strength and self-realization of our spirit, our heart, for which we exist, and if we are not receptive to life's inner beauty. Life itself propels us forward and offers new doors, as long as we avoid impeding our development with a conservative view of ourselves as a distinct component of the whole. The essence is found in collaboration, not manipulation and inner unrest.

Let us alter our inner image in such a manner that it nourishes us on the inside and provides us with the power to withstand daily temptations that undermine our confidence. Let us be receptive to the love embedded within us and not smother it, but rather embrace it as a positive force that clears away old debris that has obscured our center. Our core is a vital aspect of life that unlocks our God-given inner potentials, which enable us to embrace ourselves. Each of us opens our doors of inner bravery and power, which liberate us from whatever we don't want to be.

To be or not to be who we are is a philosophical issue, but it also symbolizes self-love, enabling us to become who we genuinely are and decide that we do not want to return. Old things compel us to follow old paths, while inner love enables us to discover what we want inside our hearts. This is a path of inner wisdom and bravery that nourishes us daily. Refrain from looking back. We have already accepted some events in the past. Be receptive to new experiences and challenges that will contribute to our inner serenity and liberate us from the past. The past can only remain in our memory if it is essential to prevent us from repeating our errors, reintroducing us to an old route or way of life that we have already outgrown with our new inner self-image.

7

Striking a Balance between Spiritulaity and Indulgence

Many people think that to be spiritual,' one must follow a rigid lifestyle. If you want to claim to be spiritual, you must adhere to a set of rules. If your goal is ascension or enlightenment, I agree that you must be completely committed and diligent.

But what about those who are just seeking a more joyful, fulfilled existence via spirituality? Should the same disciplinary measures be implemented? Although discipline is a highly valued characteristic in our culture, does it make us better or more limited? Is there a point at which discipline becomes more detrimental than beneficial?

Who said that one must be a vegetarian to be spiritual? Where is it stated that you must be spiritual to listen to soothing music? Someone just informed me that they are abstaining from sweets due to their new spiritual path. Inquiring how abstaining from sweets had anything to do with following your spiritual path, I posed the obvious question, 'Why?' The individual gave me an odd look as if to say, 'Isn't it obvious?' I never received a response since the individual went away to discuss with someone else, and the opportunity passed me by.

I also participated in a group meditation on 'indulgences' that week. You were required to consider an indulgence during the meditation. As you would guess, many things sprang to mind, ranging from reading a good book to eating a bag of chips to savouring a drink of wine, coffee, or chocolate... the list goes on and on. It brought a grin to my face, simply thinking about it. It's the little things in life that offer me the most pleasure. As I sat there laughing and feeling good about myself, the meditation began to change gears. Suddenly, I was instructed to picture myself indulging excessively in my 'indulgence.' If your pleasure is chocolate, for example, you will eat yourself sick. At this time, I was having difficulty with meditation. I allow myself many pleasures because I believe that life should be enjoyed. Additionally, I am aware from personal experience that when I give myself these pleasures and feel good about them, I never feel compelled to overindulge.

Finally, I decided to discontinue participation in this meditation since I didn't want to picture myself indulging in anything. To me, it simply didn't seem right. However, I can understand the value of this kind of meditation if you have a genuine addiction to something, something you just can not stop indulging in. The operative term here is 'excessive' indulgence. There is a significant distinction between beneficial overindulgence and hazardous overindulgence.

This is critical to grasp since believing that all pleasures are harmful to one's health is a highly imbalanced view of spirituality. I've seen that some individuals believe that by abstaining from pleasant activities, you become more spiritual. The basis for this idea is found in various faiths, which teach us that discipline and pain help us become more spiritual.

Restricting or denying oneself, in my view, does not make you more or less spiritual, nor does it expedite your spiritual journey. I think that we are here to enjoy life, not to diminish its pleasure due to our spiritual journey.

I am a firm believer in maintaining a healthy balance. For instance, I sometimes listen to hard metal music. I was first hesitant to reveal this aspect of my reality since I am aware that some spiritually oriented individuals frown upon this kind of indulgence. That is precisely why I choose to offer this nugget of knowledge. I am aware that I like it and refuse to deny it since I love and accept enough to own and feel good about this indulgence. Is this a sign that I'm becoming less spiritual? Most definitely not! It just qualifies me as someone capable of appreciating spirituality in all things.

Do I become a less centred and lucid person due to my enjoyment of a delicious steak? Most emphatically not! However, I spare a thought for the cow. Is it true that if I allow anger or irritation to emerge, I become a less loving person? Most emphatically not! We are complex people with a wide range of emotions that should be experienced, not categorized as good or evil. You are not required to repress so-called 'negative' feelings because they contradict the worldly perspective of being a spiritual person. At our heart, regardless of how we conduct our lives, we are all spiritual creatures.

If you are not seeking enlightenment, then take a balanced approach to your spiritual path. Put an end to your self-criticism just because you ate two cookies instead of one or drank a glass of wine. If you like dancing at a nightclub or reading a fantastic novel, you are not a less spiritual person.

I strive to conduct my life with these two basic principles in mind: 1. Do not cause any harm to anyone. 2. Wherever I go, I spread love and light. Everything else in life is debatable and experienceable-the decision is mine or yours.

Thus, in the spirit of spirituality, never forget to enjoy yourself and do what makes your heart sing. Remove the boundary between what it means to be spiritual and what it does not imply. Take away the judgments. They are not conducive to your greatest development. Being balanced is a great and healthy way to live.

8

We are All United in our Oneness

We are all one; we are all love; we already have everything we require...This kind of thinking maybe heard at a variety of spiritual meetings. However, are we one, and if not, do we truly want to become one? Are we grown enough to empathize with a criminal, and are we capable of empathizing with an enlightened individual?

Are we too different to complement one another, or does our variety allow us to learn from one another and complete one another? Our journey is very interesting: at first, we go from oneness to the world, where we are unaware of the oneness, to return to where we have previously been... And this process continues for many years or millennia until we achieve physical oneness and become what we have already been or have been all along but were unaware of.

In the beginning, God split Himself into an unlimited number of distinct particles and dispersed them over vast distances in the so-called Big Bang. That moment marks the beginning of oneness with all that exists. This is a knowledge that we are all descended from the same creator, God, and that we are all linked to complement and harmonize one another. However, humanity's development has led the majority of us to suppress this God particle, which unites us all, to the point that we are no longer conscious of it. This subconscious particle is a soul that resides inside our body and binds us together as a whole. However, the soul in our body has a subconscious effect on us since there is a long path ahead of us to establish a conscious connection with our soul.

Individual souls destined for manifestation on Earth form distinct groupings. They complement one another and carry out God's plan and purpose in their world. They are conscious of their oneness and work toward achieving it via mutual collaboration and harmony. When God decides that one soul will incarnate in a new life on Earth, the other souls in that soul's group establish a spiritual guiding system for that soul, which allows them to maintain their friendship and cooperation. While this soul is incarnated in a body on Earth, other souls remain in the spiritual realm and do their best to assist the incarnated soul. By doing so, they contribute to humanity's development and knowledge of oneness.

Thus, we should constantly seek spiritual advice when in need of spiritual assistance; this will assist us in progressing and evolving. Our spiritual guidance includes souls and energies with whom our soul communicates, collaborates, and co-creates a beautiful future. As we move spiritually, our spiritual direction increases and new connections are made. That is determined in God's records, and we may get greater and more intense spiritual assistance daily. The spiritual realm always provides spiritual aid. Expanded spiritual advice harmonizes and improves our existing spiritual direction, which our soul recognizes and uses to help us in our development. Some believe that everything is contained inside us, and we get nothing from the outside, yet this is just the beginning. If we continue thinking in this manner, our evolution will come to a halt. Of course, it is our decision, but given that our soul has a purpose and mission in each life, it is essential to develop in line with that purpose. Otherwise, life puts us through challenges that reintroduce us to our evolutionary path. Stagnation results in challenges we do not want to endure.

The way to convert the concept of us all being connected into something that connects us practically is to attempt a conscious connection with our soul, eventually linking us in a broader sense. Our soul is a very sheer force that is often imperceptible to the human mind. There is just one path to conscious connection. However, it is neither straightforward. First, we must recognize that our serious thoughts and negative emotions burden our bodies and mind. Our love will gradually liberate our body and spirit from all tensions and responsibilities, which is the first step. Second, we must recognize that the energy of our physical body is much lower in vibration and intensity than the energy of our soul. Thus, the only right course of action is to increase the power of our physical body to free ourselves of any emotional-mental impediments that obstruct the intake and flow of energy inside us. That is how we may gradually increase the power of our physical body to an acceptable frequency and energy level, allowing the energy of our soul and our physical body to merge. Thus, love and awareness of our spirit may be used deliberately. This is the only method that allows us to connect with our confidence in a conscious manner. All other techniques are incapable of achieving this outcome because the energy of our soul and the energy of our body are too dissimilar to form a conscious connection.

The universe is limitless and operates in perfect balance, harmony, and order. All of the universe's actions and occurrences are constantly being recorded and synced in order to maintain order, perfection, and oneness. Additionally, these records establish all spiritual hierarchies and relationships. Due to the fact that spiritual energies lack free choice, they carry out God's will through these records.

God forgives us ten times for our errors, but we must pay them back, if not in this life, then in the next. What exactly does this imply? We do both good and terrible things in our daily lives, but they generally compensate/balance out until we die. God ignores those 10 errors in order to facilitate the restitution process. If this recompense is not provided, it is made via a karmic debt that is recorded in God's karmic awareness and paid in future lifetimes through severe tribulations. If God did not forgive us for 10 errors over millennia, it is possible that our growth and advancement would be suffocated by karmic debt. God, in His infinite wisdom, predetermined the entire path of soul development, and some souls choose very different paths. While the majority of souls develop in the manner indicated above, others are exposed to and tested by lost souls, kidnapped souls, and different circumstances that obstruct and exacerbate the optimum evolution of souls. That will be discussed in one of the subsequent columns.

Often, we are unaware of how wonderful our environment is. If we are conscious of the universe's perfection, it may direct us to the correct road, the path of oneness. God desires our perfection, and it is for this reason that he gives us love that directs us toward it as we begin to see how flawless we are in our inner nature.

9

Soul Connections

We often see a variety of spiritual phrases referring to soul connections, twin souls, complementing souls, and soul mates... There are hundreds of possible answers; thus, let us examine what it all implies.

The spiritual universe is structured according to a predetermined spiritual hierarchy that may be broadly split into three levels. The first level is the astral realm, which is the spiritual hierarchy's lowest level and is designed for emotional development. The second level is mental, which is meant for mental change, and the third and final level is causal, which is intended for spiritual development. All souls residing on the three levels are referred to as terrestrial souls, since they incarnate in our physical bodies. The souls live in huge groupings of several thousand or ten thousand souls inside their own spiritual hierarchies, forming an integrated totality. All souls are mutually beneficial in all aspects of their lives and activities.

When a soul from a particular group is ready to incarnate in a human body, it does so during delivery, when the soul enters the body of a newborn infant during its first breath, thereby initiating a new phase of the body-spirit symbiosis. The other souls in the group of the newly incarnated soul will provide spiritual direction for that individual, and in this manner, the group's friendship, collaboration, and complementarity will continue. This implies that when we want to connect with the spiritual realm, we should approach our spiritual guidance, which comprises of souls from our linked group who will do all possible to ease our lives on Earth.

When two individuals with souls from the same spiritual group cross paths in physical life, they are referred to be soul mates, since the two souls are spiritual buddies. When two such individuals meet as partners in this world, it is very probable that they will collaborate and complement one another for the remainder of their lives. These linkages provide the groundwork for peaceful cohabitation, as such souls seek shared development, complementarity, and collaboration... And the two individuals are continuously attracted to one another, to a common path, to shared objectives. As a result, they are soul mates.

Complementary souls are unique. This is a phrase that refers to the meeting, existence, and cohabitation... of two individuals with souls that do not come from the same spiritual group, but carry enough energy to provide for, collaborate with, and complement one another, whether for a short period of time or their whole lives. Thus, these spirits are not connected by origin, yet their activities complement one another.

Each soul has an essential core. It is a vital component of the soul; literally, it is situated in the bottom portion of the soul, and when the soul is contained inside a body, the core is located in the heart chakra. When a person dies, the soul leaves the physical body and enters the spiritual realm with the individual's last breath; this is the point at which our inner consciousness shifts inward, into the awareness of our soul, and so establishes the foundation for subsequent lifetimes. Each life's inner awareness is a component of our soul's core, which contains all of our and our soul's records. Thus, the inner core serves as a record of our life, as well as a personification of every spiritual hierarchy inside us. Due to the fact that all lives complement, improve, and collaborate with one another, the inner core symbolises the record by which God decides a soul's future existence and establishes the location and form of the next incarnation. A soul cannot select its future existence on its own, since it lacks insight into the overarching plan for life's development on Earth. God is responsible for the universe's balance and perfection, and as a small part of this perfection, we influence the evolution of the entire humanity through our lives on a micro-level, and through our inner core, we contribute to the system of energy balancing in all the areas where we fill in a gap in our self-evolution.

However, many souls' lifetimes do overlap throughout their personal growth. If two people with souls from various spiritual levels live together as partners for three to four successive lifetimes, they ultimately develop a single inner core, since their awareness transforms into their souls' cores after death, which continues to link them in subsequent incarnations. Their souls' records include many common records, and the number of shared records increases from life to life, tying the two souls together more and more in each existence. This implies that when two individuals with similar souls cross paths, their shared core actually pulls them together, and they become inseparable companions.

When two soul mates establish a common core and spend at least a few consecutive lifetimes as lovers, their shared inner core becomes the foundation for their subsequent lives, as it gets God's commitment. A new soul is formed from the common core and is then incarnated in two bodies, implying that the soul is divided into two pieces, each of which represents a twin soul in subsequent incarnations. The soul enters the bodies of two people: when the first person is born, the whole soul enters their body; when the second person is born, a portion of the soul moves from the first to the second, symbolising an unbreakable link throughout life. A twin soul is aware of its oneness and seeks cohabitation and oneness in physical life as well.

10

New Life Secrets

Is the life we are experiencing right now all that exists, or is there more? This moment's experience is a component of our awareness that exists only in the realm we are now experiencing.

There are an infinite number of dimensions, each of which is a mirror of our energy in a multidimensional space. Temporal and space are segments of our awareness that are projected into the energy of our souls. They reflect the curve of light descending on our solar system, as they represent intermediate gaps that are not filled with time energy in the same dimensional space and time.

Dimensions are used to describe the curvature of an electromagnetic field. There are reflections of our souls in many parallel realms, illustrating our souls' varied activity. In each parallel dimension to which we are linked, our soul's awareness relives and controls emotional, mental, and spiritual elements of our existence, both past and present, and therefore affects and co-creates our future. The initial closest dimensions, which are often four, reflect our emotions' astral projection. Thus, the soul expresses our emotional reactions to previously occurring events. The following parallel dimensions reflect mental projections and mental responses to life experiences. The highest parallel dimensions are symbolic of our spiritual lives and spiritual reactions in our daily lives. These are all projections of experiences from our past incarnations, which are stored in our inner core.

In a particular section of our awareness and inner self-confidence, time symbolises the curvature of space. Additionally, it demonstrates the capacity to establish inner awareness, as it paves the way for the establishment of solid rules of interpersonal interactions, which are crystallised in our mirror image. The mirror picture reflects our current state and demonstrates our capacity to generate multidimensional activity when we operate from inside, from our inner awareness projecting old and new patterns onto astral and mental planes. They thus co-create and shape our inner view of the essence of life, which eludes us if we do not look within and seek inner peace, if we do not perceive ourselves as God's beings with a portion of the unconscious within us, within the essence of our inner core that connects all dimensions of our inner self-confidence into an integral whole and provides us with the means to live.

To simplify, we will refer to all dimensions associated with us as images. These dimensions reflect the degree of our awareness and our current development. Assume that every dimension that is linked to us is a single image. Generally, the number of images reflecting our history is equal to the number of images indicating our future. Each image is linked to the next, forming four parallel dimensions that convey the complexity of human life. Our spirits attempt to generate events in the future, images that will bring us to the road of purpose fulfilment. Souls watch all previous images and attempt to rectify our errors in future images and circumstances, which is how we achieve a balance between our good and negative acts. Prior to our death, that balance will have been reached in the majority of instances, since after death, souls are sorted into their appropriate locations depending on the inner core's present level of awareness.

Where parallel dimensions of the past and present intersect, we find our mirror image, which is the spiritual world's reflection of our awareness. Each image exists on a higher level, in a higher dimension, and when seen collectively, they form a spiral akin to a DNA helix, although they appear more like connected circles. The bottom half of the helix is rooted in our soul's deep core, while the upper half of the helix continues as a thin thread that runs across our spiritual home, or via our spiritual guidance. The thread then continues straight from our spiritual direction to God, establishing a link with God, who watches our life and directs all required spiritual assistance, guiding us through tests and tribulations to the path of God's inauguration. When we generate completely pure energy in all of our images, God's energy flows straight into our inner core, connecting us to God, who then supports us. Until all dimensions' energy is pure, obstructions will impede the flow of God's energy and spiritual assistance, which will come to a halt in the dimension where the blocks are located. When the energy is pure and unobstructed throughout, the state of awareness shown in all images reflects our blissfulness. When seen from afar, all our dimensions look like an energy beam; when viewed from a wider distance, they resemble a thread.

It is possible that we experience specific events in our dreams and so cleanse our subconscious and burdens; or that a portion of our awareness travels to one of the dimensions and relives previous occurrences, which is how we see what has to be corrected. A portion of our mind may also go into a future dimension, which is how we see essential future orientations. During profound concentration, a similar phenomenon occurs with astral projections.

When God places a soul in a body, he also determines the soul's purpose, which is our purpose in this life. Our soul's plan may also be referred to as God's inauguration of our life. A soul's purpose is to complete the given job. Following physical death, the soul returns to the spiritual realm and takes up residence in the location that corresponds to the soul's present awareness in its inner core. Michael, the Archangel, is in charge of the sorting. Naturally, if spirits did not have the ability to influence our lives, they could not be rewarded or punished for our acts in physical bodies. Parallel dimensions, on the other hand, offer exactly that possibility. What we have done incorrectly in the past is relived by our souls in the past dimensions, and in the future dimensions, they generate events and circumstances through which we will rectify all previous errors and so attain balance in our physical bodies. Our souls direct us via our emotions and may also direct us through our dreams.

We see all the qualities we want in our realisation in our inner core, but do not appear to have the power to produce them. Thus, our astral projections provide us with insight into ourselves and provide all the knowledge required for our inner peace and the establishment of God's kingdom inside us. The inner core contains evidence of God's omnipresence in all living things, as well as our inner awareness and all previous incarnations.

Peace within ourselves entails coming face to face with ourselves, with our inner core, which eludes us only when we focus only on ourselves and deviate from God's inauguration of our lives. For life itself drives us to serve others, and it is only through our collective care for one another on all levels of our existence that we can create an integrated whole that moves away from arrogance and toward love at its core.Love is the universal link that binds all living things together, uniting us as a whole.

Dimensions symbolise the way inside, into our inner consciousness, into the awareness of life itself, and they provide us with the power and hope for a better existence already in this dimension, which is the only dimension we experience as reality in daily life. Because our awareness is not multidimensional until we begin to work on ourselves, search inside, and discover the way to our inner core, which is oneness of existence on all levels and in all spheres of life. We should seek the meaning of life inside ourselves, in our inner self-confidence, and our awareness of our existence will open wide all doors to God's face, which is reflected within us at the very heart of existence.

11

Hidden Spring of Life

Someday, mankind will see one of the most significant turning moments in its history. The New Age's energy is providing new understandings of the essence of existence by offering a route of impersonal transformation of God's energy into each individual based on God's principle of reciprocity. When we submit to God's power inside us, riches beyond our wildest dreams elude us until love triumphs in our hearts. For centuries and millennia, we have been unable to establish a society based on equality, love, and equitable distribution of wealth... This watershed moment heralds the dawn of a new age and offers us a chance to live in peace, love, and equality. It is up to us whether or not we take advantage of the chance. That day marks the start of the process through which the energy of God's awareness is transformed into our own consciousness. Love will find its way into every level of our being, and it is entirely up to us to decide how our inner awareness transforms. The New Age energy is bringing serenity and tranquilly into our souls, but we must search inside and find the courage to make the necessary adjustments to continue our development. The New Age energy is God's inauguration of the new age, and it manifests the combined activity of the universe's most powerful spiritual forces. The most powerful spiritual energies are capable of spreading their energy into an endless number of dimensions, and inside each of these dimensions is God's awareness, allowing each individual component to function independently.

There are no significant bodily changes anticipated on that day; nevertheless, the day symbolises the start of an intense process of personal spiritual development. It is conceivable that the Earth's magnitude may move slightly, resulting in a change in energy during the next few days, experienced by some as a higher, more tranquil vibration, which will settle after a few days. The process that begins on that day will establish a direct link with the New Age energy, which will establish a foothold in each individual's awareness. That awareness will be present in everyone until Christmas Eve, and the link will remain with those who have changed their inner consciousness into love and who have transformed all responses based on lower emotions into love over those three days-from 21/12/2012 to 24/12/2012. That is, every incident in their daily life to which they would usually react emotionally with wrath, fear, or hate will cause them to respond with love. Thus, there is no need to meditate or pray during such days, but it is essential to organise our lives and heal the open wounds... Since spiritual steps must always be followed by physical ones, and vice versa, this is the only way to maintain an internal equilibrium between the spiritual and material worlds. Fear, hunger, rage, and hate are the apocalypses of our time, and we must begin to eradicate them from our lives now.

12

Ahead of us

Do the Atlantean period, Egypt's Golden Age, and the modern-day have anything in common? They seem to do so... The golden eras of Atlantis and Egypt were primarily defined by a high degree of spiritual development among the majority of people, whose spiritual talents developed at an amazing rate, eventually reaching near-miraculous levels. Both civilizations' secret, or more precisely, the secret of their spiritual awakening, is found in the active etheric field.

Etheric energy is the source of humanity's energy. When the greatest spiritual energies manifested physical bodies in line with God's will, etheric energy migrated out from the physical body's periphery and now encompasses the energy 10 to 15 centimetres surrounding the physical body. We have lost touch with the etheric realm as a result of our conversion to the material world and forgetting our roots. Additionally, we have lost touch with ourselves and the balance between material and spiritual life.

The physical and spiritual realms are not inextricably linked. If they were, all our dark ideas, worries, and responsibilities... would flow over to the spiritual world, upsetting the spiritual world's equilibrium as well. Two methods are currently available for establishing contact with the spiritual realm. When we are in need of assistance, spiritual forces may come to our aid subconsciously, or we may establish the connection on our own when we seek spiritual direction. Children under the age of seven have a continuous link; beyond that, the connection is severed. It is maintained exclusively for those who have a significant spiritual purpose.

Individuals who have acquired spiritual talents make use of them by connecting with their spiritual direction, which facilitates their spiritual activity. The physical body exists only to provide an energy foundation for spiritual activities. As a result, there is no need for us to engage our ego, as we are just a byproduct of the process. The ego was exactly the cause that led to the downfall of the two civilizations described above, notwithstanding their great spiritual development.

The New Age started on 21/12/2012. Numerous prophecies foretold the end of the world and other catastrophic catastrophes. However, in fact, it marked the start of a new age marked by a shift in the fundamental principles of spiritual activity. Six months prior to that day, the New Age energy subconsciously worked on the energy of people in most need of assistance. And on the actual day, the dynamic activity extended across the whole human population. However, after a week, it became apparent that the majority of individuals were not yet prepared for significant changes, since they were moving too slowly, superficially, or not at all. As a result, a quarter of individuals lost their connection to the higher frequency within one week, and the majority of others did so subsequently, due to their overwhelming load on the spiritual realm.

Around six months ago, an energy known as the White Ring developed around the Earth, representing the Earth's etheric vitality. This link was established by four of the greatest Archangels, beginning progressive changes in the Earth's frequency. Simultaneously, the process of cleansing male and female source energy started. Recently, New Age energy combined with the frequency of male and female source energy, creating circumstances conducive to the development of the etheric field in humans as well. However, spiritual energies capable of activating, purifying, and raising the frequency of a person's etheric field are rare. These are the energies that have been initiated by God to enter the etheric realm, which symbolises pure God's energy. Several of them are also spiritual energies associated with the aforementioned civilizations' spiritual activities.

Around this time, the New Age energies begin the process of cleansing the etheric fields of those who have maintained a connection to the New Age. The procedure occurs subconsciously in individuals. Physical strength will grow, general well-being will improve, and spiritual support and protection will expand. The procedure is progressive; it consists of at least four stages and lasts a full month. Following that, such folks will gradually begin to increase the vibration of others with whom they come into touch. The vitality of the rooms and places in which they will be located will also increase. Spiritual awareness and spiritual talents will eventually begin to develop.

Following that, spiritual activity will take on a new dimension. Infinite energy assistance will be provided through the etheric sphere. Spiritual energies assisting a person will remain in the etheric field for an extended period of time. Chakras, which carry spiritual energy into the physical body, will be re-calibrated. They will act as a thermostat, regulating energy circulation between the physical and etheric bodies. Of course, we must defer to spiritual forces when it comes to chakra setup. The etheric body will resemble an infinitely powerful energy storage. With time, we will be able to act with much more energy and vibration, rapidly develop our spiritual skills, and begin cooperating with one another....

Due to God's love for us and his desire for our lives to have purpose, the spiritual realm has dedicated all of its assistance to us. And it is up to us to accept that assistance, transform our core, and transform the new era into a golden age.

13

Life's Purpose

Throughout history, many great men and women have pondered the purpose of existence. This essay will go into this subject and will also prompt you to consider the purpose of your own life. I think that the meaning of life varies somewhat for each individual, since we all have unique objectives and ambitions. However, in a nutshell, we are here to further our soul's development and evolution.

Human life is very brief, and there are many temptations and diversions that may lead us astray. For instance, in the majority of instances, we need money to purchase food, clothes, and a roof over our heads. Generally, we must work for money in order to provide for ourselves and enjoy our lives. We are fortunate in the first world in that we seldom have to struggle for our existence; our fundamental necessities are generally fulfilled. However, we are often required to work a certain number of hours each week in order to meet our basic requirements. Money is just energy, and we have complete control over how we use it. Our ego is never satiated and is always on the lookout for larger and better things. Our task is also to learn to quiet our ego and balance it with the nudges of spirit.

Materialism may be a significant deterrent to spiritual development.

I've come to understand that the purpose of existence is to achieve spiritual development via teachings we select on a soul level prior to birth. While we are alive, we are endowed with free will, which means that we will not always adhere to the plan or learn our lessons. Having said that, the earth school is an excellent environment for rapid learning, and although awareness is critical, we may still absorb things subconsciously, albeit at a much slower speed. Reincarnation also contributes to our ability to reset, select anew, and continue where we left off. While our bodies are mortal at the time, our souls are eternal and will exist forever.

Because we share a collective amnesia about our soul's real beginnings and previous incarnations, it enables us to remain present and focused on our planet trip. Having some insight into our previous incarnations may help us gain a better understanding of our soul's nature and specific patterns we need to work on and perfect. This spiritual development is sometimes referred to as ascension, and it is a never-ending path of discovery and expansion. When one element of your life is mastered, another layer is brought into your conscious consciousness to concentrate on next. Another perspective on our collective development is that we are going away from fear and toward love. Numerous gurus talked about this throughout their time on earth, urging people to let go of fear and embrace love. If you are developing an unconditional love for yourself and others, you are well on your way to completing your lessons and understanding the purpose of life.

14

Five times, science and spirituality have converged

Science and spirituality do not get along very well. After all, science is concerned with describing the physical world as it can be experienced and seen instantly. Spirituality derives from explanations for the unobservable. Therefore, these two can never cross paths, correct? This is how the universe makes sense, and it's simple to pick one or the other.

Then there are the occasions when these two come together and knot at everyone's request.

These days, science scoffs at reason and calls for a more spiritual perspective. While science first alienated people from religion and the spiritual realm, recent breakthroughs in science have resulted in individuals reconnecting with their spiritual selves. Here are a few technological advancements that border on the spiritual, if not outright scary.

1. Placebo effects

Your body may completely transform based on your thinking, producing symptoms that aren't there or eradicating disease totally. In any case, the placebo effect seems to occur only when the mind is completely persuaded. While some may claim that this method might be used to treat cancer, nobody is holding their breath. However, this may have more practical implications, as one might potentially improve their exercise, lose weight quicker, boost their immune system, and feel healthier overall by just adopting and reinforcing their conviction.

2. When you die, you lose weight.

At first look, it seems to make sense. After all, don't you lose your breath and somebody's fluids when you die? However, even after accounting for breath and other bodily stuff, about 21 grammes remain unaccounted for. Duncan Mcdougall found this in 1901, and although further tests have shown that the weight fluctuates, it remains unaccounted for. Additionally, McDougall's studies show that animals, unlike humans, do not lose weight. Could this really be a "Soul"? Or do our brains even have any substance? This uncertainty becomes much more palatable when we err on the side of a "soul."

3. We are capable of photographing auras.

According to what I've read, there are a variety of things you can do with your aura. You must clean it, reinforce it, and ensure that it does not discolour the carpet. It's unsurprising that an aura is a popular target for doubters, but the finger pictures taken by John H. Slate, PhD are claimed to be aura photographs. Of course, he also discusses psychic vampires and how to combat them. Nonetheless, the aura seems to be one of the most enigmatic and intangible elements of spirituality.

4. Thoughts have an effect on water.

Dr Masaru Emoto's study demonstrates that water may be intentionally altered by thoughts and pictures. It's as though we have a larger impact than we think since water seems to take note of our presence. Water's ability to be affected may help explain why the placebo effect is so effective. After all, a large portion of our bodies are composed of water, and we are constantly releasing ideas. Suddenly, ruminating on unpleasant ideas in a body capable of "noticing" and reading them does not seem so beneficial. Indeed...

5. Numerous objects seem to take notice of us.

You may have heard of the double-slit experiment, in which the location of a particle is determined by observation. It goes much farther, though, when we are able to halt radioactive decay. When radioactive decay is halted by observation, the quantum Zeno effect occurs. When random number generators were affected, science called into question the limits of human influence. Even random number generators, scientists have discovered, may be influenced by thinking.

These are just a handful of the scientific breakthroughs that have blurred or obliterated the boundary between science and spirituality. There are scientists who assert that there is proof for phenomena such as ESP and remote seeing. Who knows what we will find next in this new era of scientific spirituality?

15

We confront our issues

When you were a child, you used to go out and play with your friends, watch cartoons and superhero movies, and then attempt to imitate your favourite hero by creating a cape for yourself out of your bath towel. We all have dreams from the moment we are born and throughout our lives. Some dreams alter with time, while others are firmly ingrained in our subconscious, propelling us toward our destiny, the person we were destined to be, and the reason for our birth.

Our world is continuously paving the path for us to discover our perfect selves. It constantly throws opportunities at our feet in a variety of ways for us to seize and transform into the superheroes we imagined. It is not physically true, but it is true in a metaphorical sense. However, growth and progress are impossible without change and process, which manifest themselves in the shape of our so-called issues, which we often avoid or attempt to overlook.

We lament our misfortune at having been selected to address these issues. At times, we even blame God for putting us through this agony. Whereas the reality is that we requested this transformational process.

Going all the way back to our infancy, we all want to be successful, unique, powerful, and intelligent men and women capable of expressing our ideas to the world and demonstrating the beauty of our interior world. While we dreamed it, hoped for it, and prayed for it, the universe listened and placed us in circumstances and with people who would assist us in becoming our unique selves. However, instead of seizing these chances, we put on our running shoes of excuses and began sprinting in the other way, unaware that our closest friend, the universe, gave us this boat of difficulties in order for us to jump on and reach the beach of success.

We are always on our way to become the person we've always desired to be. While our aspirations may evolve and evolve as we go through life, we are still attempting to be that superhero dressed in a little different outfit. Therefore, the next time you encounter a difficulty, approach it with the mindset that there is something we are missing, something we need to do differently in order to reach where we want to go. Additionally, it may be a sign that we need to push ourselves in order to surpass our perceived potential and develop into a more refined person.

16

Vulnerable Mind

"Saved by Grace"—but not without a price. I was raised as a Christian and was taught that salvation comes through embracing and experiencing God's truth. Whenever I've experienced life-changing, inner change, whether, in a Christian or non-Christian setting, it's been via an often tough but gratifying process of self-discovery. Often, the religious bells and whistles of indoctrination were a barrier to the process. Personal freedom is impossible without knowledge, which demands a sensitive curiosity about oneself and the world, as well as patient desperation for truth.

Is God going to punish this truth seeker for his ignorance? I will not embrace another's doctrine merely because it has the most frightening depiction of the hereafter for those who do not believe. If I pose the honest question, "Does God exist?"—by which I mean, the God that I was taught to believe in—will God condemn me for eternity for asking an honest inquiry? I will express that belief if I believe in my heart that God is a loving sustainer. I am not required to adorn my senses with the bells and whistles of another. Neither the paralysing dread of judgement nor the trite theft of another's truth or heroic sacrifice in exchange for a free trip to paradise, are sufficient for me.

Christ paved the way for us, but he did not do it only for the benefit of the world. He did it for his own spiritual development and kingdom. We can not just live in his shoes vicariously through belief. We are each called to bear our own cross and change ourselves. Christ's power lies not in the past but in the ever-present process of his birth, crucifixion, and resurrection inside me.

I will not stop until I have discovered wisdom—the understanding of God. Or, if you prefer, the erasure of what is false. If I have to turn over every rock to discover that none of them conceals what I'm searching for, the effort was worthwhile. I can now disregard the rocks. What was true in every culture, western or oriental, Christian or non-Christian, ancient or contemporary, remains true now. God's knowledge endures the ages. What was is no more.

I am sceptical of promised outcomes. I am not a believer in providing a method—a rigid equation—whether in the shape of a religion or a specific practice, but I think that all "equations" are worth studying in order to understand their roots and why they were employed. Even worse would be to promise an individual's particular outcome from such treatment. The spiritual endeavour of an individual has far too many variables: motivations, expectations, desires, personality, talents, and so forth. The most wonderful things that happen to us are unanticipated. Life arrived without an instruction manual (until someone gave one to us), and we were delighted at every step. When we were children, we had no previous experiences to draw from. This is why, especially in spirituality, we can benefit from prior experiences but must approach Spirit with a pure, childish curiosity.

We require a new, yet ancient, vision of spirituality that is zealous for truth but not presumptuous—a spirit that is not afraid of its own vulnerability in the face of the unknown, nor of the Unknown itself... a spirit that is not satisfied with the pat answers offered by our ego's rationalisations or by spiritual leaders and their conventionally accepted interpretations of scriptures.

A fragile spirit is not unprotected. If your only protection is acceptance of what your conscious mind has acquired from birth—certain techniques, customs, and beliefs—then you have none. A spirit that confronts the world in which it finds itself with true curiosity, courageous humility, wide-eyed at dazzling brightness, and a willingness to explore the deepest recesses... this spirit may encounter hardship, upheaval, and confusion, but will not fear divine judgement. Rather than that, this attitude is heroic and will reap the benefits of heroism.

Traditional spiritual standards are eroding. Previously acceptable answers by people seeking simple security via religion are no longer accepted. Religious fanaticism and banal secularism are increasingly revealing their flaws. Faith is being tried, but "faith," or more precisely, belief, is being revealed as a fake.

Answers. Answers. Answers. The simpleton seeks answers from other seeming human brains. Being a truth seeker entails desiring answers but understanding that they do not come easily. This "simplicity" is everything but. Accepting another's spiritual response can only result in disappointment and complication. The most significant "answers" emerge from in-depth personal investigation into the unknown.

17

Appreciationg a man for who he is

Although it is said that laughter is the best medicine, I am sceptical. I'm discovering that laughter without joy is merely a diversion, a means of removing myself from the overwhelming emotion that occasionally grips me. What I am discovering is that joy is what enables me to move mountains. The joy of witnessing random acts of kindness, where someone who is distraught is suddenly rescued by another person who merely cares. Not someone repairing, not someone guiding, but the simple act of someone sitting next to another to alleviate isolation. At these points, tears stream down my cheeks.

Recently, something occurred that has stayed with me. I was at my oncologist's office for my semi-annual visit. My oncologist specialises in neck and head cancers. Cancer in the head region can be one of the most intrusive conditions to observe, let alone live with. Many cancers allow us to conceal our scars and disfigurement. However, cancers of the face and head cannot be concealed, and tumours protrude forth in vile acknowledgement of illness.

My Oncologist's waiting room can feel like an elevator; patients grab magazines to divert their attention and engage in distraction dances to avoid each other's gaze. It's uncomfortable, but it's also dehumanising for both the recipient and the giver of blank stares.

That day, directly across from me stood a man with a monstrous tumour that had grown to cover his left eye and down his cheek. To say it was confronting would be an understatement. I peered and saw his wife clutching his arm, I'm sure to show him the love he so desperately needed and to protect her from the fear I'm sure she felt at the prospect of losing him.

I quickly shuffled through the pages of a business magazine, attempting to avoid eye contact, but something overcame me, and I looked up and directly at him. It didn't take long to pique his interest. I simply smiled and then blurted out, "Be careful in there; he enjoys pretending to be a proctologist." If he approaches you from your blind side, he may be planning something".

You could hear a pin drop, and then he looked back and softened his one eye, forming a tear, and he began to smile broadly. We shared a few moments of laughter and then simply exchanged personal space. Apart from his wife and medical professionals, I believe I was the first person in a long time to see him as a person, not a disease.

We discussed each other's illnesses and treatments, politics, sports, and whatever else came up; it didn't matter; we simply talked. He was the first to enter the Oncologist's office, and we all nodded as he entered. He emerged a few moments later, smiling at me and making a gesture as if the doctor had inspected his rear. He smiled, I smiled, and for those brief moments, we were nothing more than friends.

The most touching part was when, as he walked out of the office, his wife returned my gaze and simply mouthed "thank you." I shook my head as if to say, "Why?" After my appointment, I drove to the parking garage and sat in my car, crying. It washed over me like a tidal wave of emotion – the exchanged moment of joy was the most powerful thing that had happened to me in a long time. But it wasn't because I was a hero or pushed myself beyond my comfort zone; it was because a brave man allowed me in and allowed me to see his vulnerability, and in doing so, I discovered we shared a sense of humour about fate.

Because of that day, I know one truth: it takes courage to reach out to someone who is hurting. However, allowing someone in and being open takes an enormous amount of courage. That day, I received a blessing from the most courageous man I've encountered in a long time.

I connected that day, and despite the fact that I was alone on the drive home, I was not alone. Namaste, my friends; may you welcome someone in and bestow upon them a wonderful gift.

18

Through your professional goal

With the expansion of churches and different ministries, leadership roles have expanded as well, with many pursuing positions and power at the cost of the flock, which has been left stranded with no one to assist them in finding their talent and service in the body of Christ.

The church is in trouble because leaders have become fixated on what they can get rather than on what they can offer. Many have migrated from church to church in search of positions of power and control; others have been appointed worship leaders with little understanding of what worship is. Prayer and bible study has been pushed to the side as many compete for jobs regardless of their calling. Indeed, the struggle for dominance is akin to that which occurs in a political arena.

I attended a church recently for a Sunday service and was taken aback when the programmer stated that it was leadership election week, encouraging candidates to campaign and persuade people to elect them. More unexpected was when each candidate was given five minutes at the pulpit to promote his or her ideas and the value he or she would bring to the assigned ministry position.

As I thought about this, I understood that working in any ministry is about more than titles; it is about the effect we have on others. Whether you're serving as an usher or making tea for the visitors, everything you're doing is a service to God that we must perform wholeheartedly. We cannot move from one field of service to another in order to get recognition; rather, we must stay loyal to our calling.

Thus, the Twelve assembled all the disciples and said, "It would not be proper for us to abandon the ministry of the word of God in order to wait tables." Choose seven men from among you who are known to be filled with the Spirit and knowledge, brothers and sisters. We shall delegate this duty to others and devote our time to prayer and word ministry." 2-4, Act 6: (new international version)

The scriptures demonstrate that the disciples could not have accomplished everything simultaneously; they understood their area of responsibility, and the ministry of serving at the tables had to be assigned to those who could be more successful. It was not about titles or positions of authority, but about fulfilling the needs of Christians and edifying the body of Christ. Even resigning from your present position in a ministry is more advantageous if it does not result in development for those reporting to you.

Lord, assist me in staying loyal to my purpose so that I may serve you joyfully and with inner fulfilment. Allow me to be a vessel of service in the work for which you have created me. Amen.

Twenty-one. Explosive Spirituality: Not all awakenings are peaceful. This Christmas, how many New Age books did you gift or receive? How many do you currently have on your bookshelves? Is it possible to coerce a spiritual awakening?

THEY SPEAK OF EPIC JOURNEYS BEGINNING WITH A SINGLE STEP, but I'm not convinced. The more I consider it, the more persuaded I am that the most epic trips are seldom planned in advance; rather, they unfold over weeks, months, years, and decades. Perhaps even throughout a lifetime. Steve Jobs, Apple's founder, put it best when he compared life to a 'connect the dots' exercise. While the trip and path seem apparent in hindsight, while you are standing in the dotty chaos of life, you must believe that as you leap, skip, or struggle from dot to dot, they will eventually join meaningfully. It's all about trust.

However, trust is a peculiar notion. We trust organisations more than the individuals inside them-consider banks and bankers-and brands more than the goods that bear their mark-consider Coca-Cola and Coke. We place a higher premium on the advisors and counsellors we hire than on ourselves. Why do you believe that is the case?

Inevitably, trust in a higher force (your God, Spirit, or the Universe) is given too readily or not at all. This is most likely true of our trust and confidence in ourselves. We either put it incorrectly or not at all. What would it be like to have complete confidence in ourselves, our environment, and our position within it? There is no self-consciousness or impostor syndrome. How would that even appear? I lack your understanding, yet I think that it would resemble serenity; personal peace. And how far might this inner calm go if such trust took hold in this viral age? Perhaps to our families, to our communities, to our nation, and perhaps even worldwide. Is this oversimplified? Perhaps, but perhaps not. However, I am reminded of Malala's icon status and the power of one.

power. How at ease are you with reading that word? What does the term "power" mean to you? What associations does it evoke in your mind: corruption, riches, bad or good?Personally, I accept power to be the internal flame that fires my soul anytime I follow my guidance. When this power activates, I feel a tangible, chest-expanding explosion that tingles my whole body to the point that my fingers begin to shake. The physical sensation and energy are so intense that I can feel sparks emanating from my fingers, as if I could ignite a fire with my fingertips alone.

Twice in my adult life, I have lost sight of my own strength. That is now something I understand and embrace. I think that we are all born radiant, but that life's difficulties wear us down and cause us to lose sight of our inherent, unique strength. Our lives may dim our light, making it harder to see clearly. We need illumination. The world needs both mine and your light. A significant part of our mission in this lifetime must undoubtedly be to safeguard our inner light and to prevent that inside flame from dying completely.

When it occurred for the first time, my life became a state of triage, with many people intervening and attempting to assist. Never speak about me to me. Non-emergency issues were neglected; emergency issues were addressed with patches and sticky tape, but nothing was cured. How could this have happened? Nothing was resolved, and, more disappointingly, nothing was discovered. This massive crisis point sent my life tumbling down around me, yet I rejected any attempts at reform, healing, and assistance. By clinging to my shattered existence, I denied myself the chance for a new, simpler, and better life. All the lovely possibilities for learning lessons and releasing destructive habits vanished. I rose to my feet and hobbled over the next several years. It would be almost a decade before the chance arose again.

As with the first time, the second time did not feel like an opportunity. It seemed as if my world was crumbling once again, except this time I lacked the strength to even attempt to hold on. I was exhausted; my spirit ached with exhaustion. To be really candid, I felt shattered. There are many ways to describe this time; it was more than just a rough patch; it was rock bottom.I was enduring my soul's terrible night.

For the first time in my life, I realised that I lacked the ability to fight. And, although I was unaware at the time, this would prove to be my saving grace. The benefit of reaching rock bottom is that there is nothing further to go. As a result, there was no mask to maintain this time, no denial, no evasion of truth. Nowhere is more real than rock bottom, and that conviction became my saviour at a period of whirling uncertainty. Adversity may serve as an effective launch pad. Gone is the pride that refuses assistance; gone is the fear of failure; gone is the ego-protecting, face-saving nonsense with which we humans are so fond (and which I was particularly adept at). It was completely depleted. And, most surprisingly, I discovered a sort of serenity in its stead, but it was peace via explosion. It served as a reminder that not all awakenings are peaceful. By accepting whatever assistance or comfort offered, I encountered love in a manner that made me wonder whether I had been experiencing it up to this point. I saw the value of compassion, both for myself and for others. Through all of this, which took months, came clarity, which altered everything.

Any reader of self-help books or New Age spiritual teachings is aware that forgiveness, compassion, empathy, and love are necessary tools for overcoming negative ideas and emotions of blame, guilt, or victimisation. However, this does not always come easy. It may be challenging to conceive or visualise spreading waves of love to others when the emotion is not genuine. What I've discovered so far on my trip (which hasn't gone very far at all) is that it all starts with love.

All healing is possible with love, since compassion is simply a by-product or symptom of that love. And when compassion is present, blame begins to dissipate. Without guilt, the need for forgiveness dissipates. I wish I could pinpoint the exact time in my trip when I first felt love. I knew within a day or two of it occurring because I had the greatest sensations of light-headedness, explosive euphoria, serenity, and something I can only describe as chest-expanding. None of these emotions were familiar six months before, and I knew that transformative change was imminent. While I was shocked, I was not surprised. This is what I had requested, what I had sought, and upon which I had pondered. Why are we taken aback when we get what we request? I had the sensation of vibrating, and not only on an energetic level, but also physically. My hands were making sweeping motions as if to expel this sensation. I wanted everyone to feel it. I'm not sure when or when my spiritual path began, but I recall purchasing CDs for anger release more than a decade ago. If only I'd known what I know now back then. The additional information is necessary, but it is not the solution. The solution is love. And I am certain of this. Therefore, while I am learning, if there is one thing I can teach you, let it be love. First and first, love yourself and everyone else; everything else will come.

19

The Silence Lesson

Silence teaches us to view our lives and hearts for what they really are. Numerous people walk across the stage of life like untrained actors reading hollow lines placed in their mouths by other allegedly authoritarian individuals or the contents of shallow writings by others, never truly understanding they simply live their assigned roles according to materialistic society's dictates, avoiding a close examination of who they truly are on the inside. It is much simpler to succumb to the brashness, frantic speed, and confusion of the outside world.

However, when you take a step back, stop, and allow yourself to enter the regions of stillness, the actor's part is taken away, revealing the beauty of quiet and the unproven heart's lie.

The more times this is repeated until it becomes a daily holy deed, the more the wonder, richness, and holiness of your inner universe fill your existence. This is the actual condition of grace and truth, from which your whole existence flows like a clear stream. It is in this condition of profound stillness that one gradually gains mastery over one's life and destiny, no longer subject to the vagaries and fickleness of outer physical existence.

It is not by accident or whim that so many great people of the past withdrew from the world and their jobs for periods of time; they recognised the immense importance and need for quiet, as well as its ability to rejuvenate and re-energise the body, mind, and soul.

Over the centuries, humanity has lost the basic fact that all forms, all of creation, from a stone to a star, originated in the depths of cosmic stillness. Whether the seed of a plant germinates in the dark soil or the seed of a star-world germinates in the depths of the cosmos, that birth occurs in the depths of endless stillness without exception.

Inspiration is the voice of the Soul—the "Mind and Consciousness of God" that imbues each human being with life and intelligence. The most reliable protection against deadly mistakes is the intelligent development of the gift of inspiration. The explanation is self-evident; mistakes are impossible at the soul level; this is the realm of pure light.

For individuals desiring to discover their innate divinity, the ultimate task is to elevate the mortal via a true process of spiritual alchemy. This enables man to mirror the unerring knowledge and illumination of the soul in thought, speech, and deed without distortion or departure.

Bibliography

The Art of Letting Go. (2021). The-Guided-Meditation-Site.com. https://www.the-guided-meditation-site.com/the-art-of-letting-go.html

Unconditionally Loving Our Human Needs. (2021). The-Guided-Meditation-Site.com. https://www.the-guided-meditation-site.com/unconditionally-loving-our-human-needs.html

INNER SELF - IMAGE. (2021). The-Guided-Meditation-Site.com. https://www.the-guided-meditation-site.com/inner-self-image.html

WE ARE ALL ONENESS. (2021). The-Guided-Meditation-Site.com. https://www.the-guided-meditation-site.com/we-are-all-oneness.html

Soul connections. (2021). The-Guided-Meditation-Site.com. https://www.the-guided-meditation-site.com/soul-connections.html

New Secrets of Life, part 2. (2012). The-Guided-Meditation-Site.com. https://www.the-guided-meditation-site.com/new-secrets-of-life-part-2.html

New Secrets of Life, part 1. (2012). The-Guided-Meditation-Site.com. https://www.the-guided-meditation-site.com/new-secrets-of-life-part-1.html

A Father and a Dog: Two spirit guides. (2021). The-Guided-Meditation-Site.com. https://www.the-guided-meditation-site.com/a-father-and-a-dog-two-spirit-guides.html

What does the future hold for us? (2012). The-Guided-Meditation-Site.com. https://www.the-guided-meditation-site.com/what-does-the-future-hold-for-us.html

What Is The Meaning of Life?A Spirit Inspired View. (2021). The-Guided-Meditation-Site.com. https://www.the-guided-meditation-site.com/what-is-the-meaning-of-life-a-spirit-inspired-view.html

5 times Science and Spirituality met up. (2021). The-Guided-Meditation-Site.com. https://www.the-guided-meditation-site.com/5-times-science-and-spirituality-met-up.html

why we should face our problems. (2021). The-Guided-Meditation-Site.com. https://www.the-guided-meditation-site.com/why-we-should-face-our-problems.html

Vulnerable Mind : Free Spirit. (2021). The-Guided-Meditation-Site.com. https://www.the-guided-meditation-site.com/vulnerable-mind-free-spirit.html

Seeing a Man as He is. (2021). The-Guided-Meditation-Site.com. https://www.the-guided-meditation-site.com/seeing-a-man-as-he-is.html

Remaining true in your vocation. (2021). The-Guided-Meditation-Site.com. https://www.the-guided-meditation-site.com/remaining-true-in-your-vocation.html

Explosive Spirituality: Not all awakening is gentle. (2021). The-Guided-Meditation-Site.com. https://www.the-guided-meditation-site.com/explosive-spirituality-not-all-awakening-is-gentle.html

Accepting all of you!! (2017). The-Guided-Meditation-Site.com. https://www.the-guided-meditation-site.com/accepting-all-of-you.html

The Lesson of Silence. (2021). The-Guided-Meditation-Site.com. https://www.the-guided-meditation-site.com/the-lesson-of-silence.html

Trusting Your Intuition. (2021). The-Guided-Meditation-Site.com. https://www.the-guided-meditation-site.com/trusting-your-intuition.html

Human Destiny & Your Life PathQ & A with Brad Austen. (2021). The-Guided-Meditation-Site.com. https://www.the-guided-meditation-site.com/human-destiny-your-life-path-q-a-with-brad-austen.html

What Is The Meaning of Life?A Spirit Inspired View. (2021). The-Guided-Meditation-Site.com. https://www.the-guided-meditation-site.com/what-is-the-meaning-of-life-a-spirit-inspired-view.html

Channeling - How To Discern Truth From Fiction. (2021). The-Guided-Meditation-Site.com. https://www.the-guided-meditation-site.com/channeling-how-to-discern-truth-from-fiction.html

What Does It Mean To Be Free? (2012). The-Guided-Meditation-Site.com. https://www.the-guided-meditation-site.com/what-does-it-mean-to-be-free.html

Ascension - A Higher-Self PerspectiveQ & A with Brad Austen. (2021). The-Guided-Meditation-Site.com. https://www.the-guided-meditation-site.com/ascension-a-higherself-perspective-q-a-with-brad-austen.html

Free Will Versus Divine Will. (2021). The-Guided-Meditation-Site.com. https://www.the-guided-meditation-site.com/free-will-versus-divine-will1.html

Many Paths To Enlightenment. (2021). The-Guided-Meditation-Site.com. https://www.the-guided-meditation-site.com/many-paths-to-enlightenment1.html

Have a Little Faith. (2021). The-Guided-Meditation-Site.com. https://www.the-guided-meditation-site.com/have-a-little-faith.html

Life Was Made For Joy And Woe - A Lesson In Acceptance. (2021). The-Guided-Meditation-Site.com. https://www.the-guided-meditation-site.com/life-was-made-for-joy-and-woe-a-lesson-in-acceptance.html

9 798886 842012

Printed by Libri Plureos GmbH in Hamburg, Germany